HOW TO RAISE AND TRAIN A GERMAN WIREHAIRED POINTER

By Newton L. Compere

Distributed in the U.S.A. by T.F.H. Publications, Inc., 211 West Sylvania Avenue, P.O. Box 27, Neptune City, N.J. 07753; in England by T.F.H. (Gt. Britain) Ltd., 13 Nutley Lane, Reigate, Surrey; in Canada by Clarke, Irwin & Company, Clarwin House, 791 St. Clair Avenue West, Toronto 10, Ontario; in Southeast Asia by Y. W. Ong, 9 Lorong 36 Geylang, Singapore 14; in Australia and the south Pacific by Pet Imports Pty. Ltd., P.O. Box 149, Brookvale 2100, N.S.W., Australia.
Published by T.F.H. Publications, Inc. Ltd., The British Crown Colony of Hong Kong.

Cover painting courtesy of the author: A magnificent pair of German Wirehaired Pointers in the field.

Frontispiece: Ch. Oldmill Flint, owned by Dr. U. D. Mostosky and bred by the author. Sire: Ch. Oldmill Casanova; dam: Heidi of Oldmill. This dog's expression is typical of the warm kindliness that is a part of this versatile breed.

Photo Credits

Evelyn Shafer, 5; E. Münch, 8, 9, 10, 11; Ted Ritter, 12, 25, 26, 27; William Gilbert, 13; Joan Ludwig, 15; Frasie Studios, 17; Cain Fotos, 20.

ISBN 0-87666-304-8

Contents

I. History, Description and Standard

APPEARANCE AND TEMPERAMENT

The German Wirehaired Pointer, formerly known as the *German Drahthaar*, is a medium-sized dog, but is one of the largest of the pointing breeds. Without a doubt, the most outstanding identifying features are the coat and the furnishings on the head. The muzzle has bushy whiskers and there is a beard on the lower jaw, while the eyes are protected by bushy brows. These unusual head furnishings give the viewer the impression of a gruff old man or a bearded clown.

German Wirehaired Pointers range in color from solid liver to mostly white with liver spots and ticking. The head is always liver, sometimes with

Ch. Flint's Missy (left) and Ch. Flint's Chip, winning best of opposite sex and best of breed respectively at the Detroit Kennel Club under judge N. L. Compere. Missy's handler is Virginia Hardin, while Flint is being shown by Barbara Humphries.

5

a white blaze that may start between the eyes and run back over the top of the head. The white coloring on the body is usually ticked with liver, giving the coat a roan appearance. The whiskers on the muzzle may be brown, liver, reddish, or white.

The typical German Wirehaired Pointer puppy has endless energy and is doing something all of the time. He is extremely inquisitive—combine this with his endless energy, and you have quite a package! He is very affectionate, and is always on hand for that extra pat on the head. I have found that he will put his head under your hand for an extra amount of petting almost any time he sees that you are not doing something else. Affection: yes, he thrives on it!

The breed as a whole is extremely desirous to please; this trait is obvious through the various stages of puppyhood, and continues through their adult lives. A professional field-trainer who has field-trained many German Wirehaired Pointers has said that, on the average, the German Wirehaired Pointer is the easiest of the Continental Pointers to train because of this strong desire to please. Coupled with this desire, however, is a certain amount of "Germanic stubbornness."

Oldmill's Spice with one of the first litters of German Wirehairs that achieved A.K.C. recognition. Among others this litter contained Ch. Oldmill's Casanova, one of the greats of the breed in the United States.

This youngster, by Oldmill Kennebeck out of Freyja v. Dietrichstein, is already showing that she will possess the proper double coat at maturity. She was bred by Dr. and Mrs. A. J. Bartoli.

Wirehairs often want to "do it their way," instead of the way that you want the particular job done. They learn readily, once this stubbornness is overcome. Willy Necker, the renowned trainer, has used a German Wirehaired Pointer in his retrieving act for many years. In this act the dog is used to perform some most unusual and difficult routines.

The dogs make excellent housepets, as they enjoy being with their owners. They thrive on the companionship of children. When necessary, they will unhesitatingly protect their own; but at the same time, they are not prone to make an unprovoked attack. In Germany they are considered to be aloof, but not unfriendly; this so-called aloofness, as a trait, does not seem to have followed the breed to this country. All of the dogs that I have known have responded with a wagging tail to an extended, friendly hand.

ORIGIN AND HISTORY IN EUROPE

The breed, as indicated by its name, had its origin in Germany, from whence it spread to other northern European countries. The breed, known as Drahthaar in Germany, is translated in English as Wirehaired, thus the American name of German Wirehaired Pointer.

The German sportsman demands from his dog that it be able to work as an all-arounder. The dog must be able to find game, and point game as well as retrieve the wounded and killed. It must work the thickets on command, track, and trail, as well as retrieve in water. The dogs, with appropriate training, must work equally well with game birds, rabbits, fox, deer, and boar. In the 1870's, it was recognized that the all-around sporting dog was missing; hence, the effort to create the all-around sporting dog.

It had to be a dog that combined the good abilities of the Pointer; its speed, fine nose, and staunch pointing, with the desired traits of liking water, trailing skills, retrieving abilities, intelligence and ease of training. Furthermore, the dog had to be hardy and persevering. Because of the last requirement, it was considered necessary that the dog be rough-coated, because a coarse and wiry coat would give the best protection against weather, damage by thorns, bushes, and rushes, to make it useful for hunting in any terrain and in all seasons.

In the beginning, the Griffon and Stichelhaar afforded the general type of coat that was considered most desirable; however, these breeds had been

There exists, within the German Wirehaired Pointer breed, five basic types. This animal is typical of the Odin type, the most prevalent in the background of American animals.

bred more for exhibitions than performance, and many of the desired abilities were lacking. Here, the Pudel Pointer was introduced, since he added the abilities of the Pointer, as well as the high degree of intelligence and sporting abilities of the Poodle. The German Shorthaired Pointer was also used to intensify the pointing instincts.

On May 15, 1902, the *Varein Deutsch Drahthaar* (German Wirehaired Club) was formed in Berlin. This organization included persons interested in all rough-coated sporting dogs. The motto of the club could have been, "Breed as you like, create progress, and tell honestly what you have used." This club was fortunate in that the right men were on top. They were experienced, skilled breeders and sportsmen who made great contributions toward breed improvement. Lauffo Unkel am Rhein was president from the start and continued in that office for the following 32 years.

The purpose of the club was put into words as follows: *The first thing to be obtained is perfection in hunting, next a good and suitable build, and finally beauty.* It did not take long before the first goal was reached, because of the liberty that was given in breeding, which included the use of Pudel Pointers, Stichelhaars, Griffons, and Shorthairs. The second and third goals were more difficult to reach. But, after some years, more and more dogs appeared with a correct conformation. The hair was, and still is, the most difficult

The Witboi type.

The Lump type.

point. The necessity to be very critical in choice and to use only the best in breeding was of utmost importance. To control this, rules were made and are still in effect, that the dogs could only be registered in the *Stammbuch Deutsch Drahthaar* (German Wirehaired Studbook) after the age of one year (later reduced to seven months), and that the dog's coat and conformation must be approved, as well as its abilities in the field. In the German Hunting-dog Studbook there were more Wirehairs (Drahthaars) entered in 1923 than Shorthairs, and they have led in this position ever since.

The fight for recognition was hard and long, and not until 1928, after the Wirehairs had held the leading position in registrations for sporting dogs, did the German Wirehaired Club gain membership in the German Kartell for dogs.

It was finally commonly recognized that the German Wirehaired Club had reached its goal to develop a rough-coated sporting dog that answered the sportsman's all-around demands. Many sportsmen today have varied sporting grounds, which include common field shooting of birds and rabbits, as well as wooded shooting of birds and fur-bearing animals, plus the shooting of waterfowl over marshes and open water. The Wirehair has proven itself to be a dog that could be used for all these types of hunting.

Today hunting is not for sustenance, nor should it be a contest. There

The Harras Type.

The Regent type.

must be responsibility to the nation not to decrease wild game, and responsibility to the game that it not suffer needlessly. Hunting is not gentle, but it must not become beastly. The first responsibility demands careful and sensible shooting. The second demands of the sportsman that he have a dog of sufficient abilities and training to avoid losing wounded or killed game. The searching, finding and retrieving, on command, of game is the prime consideration of any sporting dog, and the Wirehair has proven its capabilities in all hunting situations.

The correct breeding of Wirehairs is absolutely not easy, especially the breeding of a correct coat. This problem can be readily understood when one realizes that the breed has a background of varied ancestors, with varied coats of smooth and wooly hair. We still find, mostly where careless breeding is done, varying and undesirable coats like sleek-haired, or wooly-haired. In the European countries, a study has been made of this problem and great care has been given to the seeking out of solutions. A similar program must be followed in the United States in order to preserve the quality and to maintain the standards of the breed. The German Wirehaired Pointer has reached

Ch. Oldmill Shenandoah, owned by Mrs. Charles Hyde. He is shown with his handler, Robert Walgate.

Ch. Talbach's Maximillian, owned and handled by Margaret Wolontis. This handsome male has made some nice wins in good competition. He is shown here winning the breed at the Lehigh Valley Kennel Club under judge Reed F. Hankwitz.

the pinnacle in Germany and, with time, should reach a similar position among the sporting dogs in America.

THE GERMAN WIREHAIRED POINTER IN AMERICA

The first German Drahthaars were brought to the United States in the early 1920's, but their numerical strength was very low. This situation did not change until after World War II. Many American servicemen had seen the dogs perform in the field: they were obviously pleased with what they had seen, for many of them made arrangements to have dogs brought to the United States. Since the 1940's many dogs have been imported from Denmark, Germany, and Sweden. The Hagenwald Tests, which are held annually in Germany to test the ability of the dogs as well as grade them in conformation, are an excellent place from which to start in choosing a dog to bring to this country. In these tests the dogs are graded for pointing, retrieving, and tracking.

The German Drahthaar Club of America (now known as the German Wirehaired Pointer Club of America) was formed by a group of ten interested Chicagoans in 1950. In addition to this club, there are, at present, breed clubs in California, Illinois, and Wisconsin.

The German Drahthaar Pointer Club of America first petitioned the American Kennel Club for breed recognition in 1955. At this time pedigrees of approximately two hundred dogs were submitted. Of these about 75 were of dogs that had been imported from Germany and Denmark—the balance were American-bred dogs. Unfortunately, some of the imported dogs were not accepted; hence, any American-bred dogs stemming from them were not accepted for registration by the American Kennel Club.

The reasons for the failure for some of the dogs to be accepted by the Kennel Club were clearly marked on the import pedigrees. The policy which had been established by the Varein Deutsch Drahthaar in 1902—namely, "Breed as you like, and tell honestly what you have used" —is where the problem arose, as far as the American Kennel Club was concerned. In first establishing the breed, the cross-breeding of Griffons, Stichelhaars, Pudel Pointers, and German Shorthaired Pointers was used. It is not uncommon for one of these registered breeds to show up on the pedigree of an imported Deutsch Drahthaar. This policy of cross-breeding has been dropped in Denmark. The German pedigrees will indicate, as well as the registration numbers, breeds of all dogs shown in the pedigree (Deutsch Drahthaar= D.D., German Shorthaired Pointer=D.K., Pudel Pointer=P.P., Stichelhaar =Stk.). Cross-breeding in Germany is not an arbitrary thing by any matter, but is done for specific purposes: a particular bloodline may be used to enhance pointing instincts, retrieving instincts, and tracking abilities. The Varein Deutsch Drahthaar has particular stud dogs which are recommended in their particular specialty: upland game, water fowl, deer tracking, hare tracking and trailing, and boar hunting. The breeders in Germany are told which studs they are to use after a thorough examination of pedigree, conformation, and abilities has been made.

As far as the American Kennel Club is concerned, in addition to the problem of cross-breds (which they will not register), there is the problem of color. In Germany, perhaps thirty percent of the dogs have black coloring. They may be black, black and white, or black with ticking. The color black is unacceptable for registration by the American Kennel Club! Perhaps, at some future date, when the reasons for the black color are more fully explained by the Varein Deutsch Drahthaar to the American Kennel Club, the latter may change its rulings concerning the color black.

Finally, after four years, the German Drahthaar was accepted for registration by the American Kennel Club. In making this new recognized breed, the name was Americanized. Drahthaar means "Wirehaired," hence German Wirehaired Pointer was the name chosen. There are many dogs that were not

Jennums Riss (left) and Bredballergards Kay, kennelmates, scoring together at the same show. Both dogs are owned by Dr. Robert Cockcroft.

Ch. Balder v. Dietrichstein, owned by Dr. G. Sewall. He is shown in a win under judge Haskell Schuffman at the Harbor Cities Kennel Club.

accepted for registration by the American Kennel Club that were registered, and are still registered, by the American Field. To be certain that you are getting what you want, insist on a registration certificate from the American Kennel Club in addition to one offered by the American Field, should only the registration be offered.

There has never been a great number of the breed exhibited at dog shows, as the large percentage of the dogs were purchased for their field abilities by persons who wanted hunting dogs. The National Specialty for German Wirehaired Pointers has, until 1966, been held in conjunction with the International Kennel Club Show in Chicago. At this particular dog show a person will have the opportunity to see perhaps twenty of these dogs at one time.

The field trials of the Continental Pointers (German Shorthairs, Weimaraners, and Vizslas), as well as some Pointer and Setter trials, have been open to the German Wirehaired Pointers since the late 1940's. As a result of the participation in field trials held under the auspices of the American Field, prior to 1959, when the breed was recognized by the American Kennel Club, the dogs were immediately acceptable for the licensed field trials held by many clubs in the Midwest. The German Wirehaired Pointer Club has for many years sponsored its own trials. These trials have encompassed pointing and retrieving of upland game birds as well as the retrieving of waterfowl. These trials have been in many instances open to all comers. The German Wirehaired Pointers have usually held their own in all phases of the sport—with Pointers and with Retrievers. Yes, they are an all-around hunting dog!

STANDARD OF THE GERMAN WIREHAIRED POINTER

The German Wirehaired Pointer is a dog that is essentially Pointer in type, of sturdy build, lively manner, and an intelligent, determined expression. In disposition the dog has been described as energetic, rather aloof but not unfriendly.

Head—The head is moderately long, the skull broad, the occipital bone not too prominent. The stop is medium, the muzzle fairly long with nasal bone straight and broad, the lips a trifle pendulous but close and bearded. The nose is dark brown with nostrils wide open, and the teeth are strong with scissors bite. The ears, rounded but not too broad, hang close to the sides of the head. Eyes are brown, medium in size, oval in contour, bright and clear and overhung with bushy eyebrows. Yellow eyes are not desirable. The neck is of medium length, slightly arched and devoid of dewlap, in fact, the skin throughout is notably tight to the body.

Body and Tail—The body is a little longer than it is high, as ten is to nine, with the back short, straight and strong, the entire back line showing a perceptible slope down from withers to croup. The chest is deep and capa-

16

Ch. Oldmill's Casanova made breed history by being the first German Wirehaired Pointer to win a best in show. He made this win at the Owensboro Kennel Club under judge Charles M. Siever. This dog is owned by the author and was handled by him here.

cious, the ribs well sprung, loins taut and slender, the tuck-up apparent. Hips are broad, with croup nicely rounded and the tail docked, approximately two-fifths of original length.

Legs and Feet—Forelegs are straight, with shoulders obliquely set and elbows close. The thighs are strong and muscular. The hind legs are moderately angulated at stifle and hock and as viewed from behind, parallel to each other. Round in outline, the feet are webbed, high arched with toes close, their pads thick and hard, and their nails strong and quite heavy. Leg bones are flat rather than round, and strong, but not so heavy or coarse as to militate against the dog's natural agility.

Coat—The coat is weather resisting and to some extent water repellent. The undercoat is dense enough in winter to insulate against the cold but so thin in summer as to be almost invisible. The distinctive outer coat is straight, harsh, wiry and rather flat-lying, from one and one-half to two inches in length, it is long enough to protect against the punishment of rough cover but not so long as to hide the outline. On the lower legs it is shorter and

This photograph shows the correct coat length over the withers. The coat of a German Wirehair should always be abundant enough to protect the dog against brambles and similar materials in the field.

between the toes of softer texture. On the skull it is naturally short and close fitting, while over the shoulders and around the tail it is very dense and heavy. The tail is nicely coated particularly on the underside, but devoid of feather. These dogs have bushy eyebrows of strong, straight hair and beards and whiskers of medium length.

A short smooth coat, a soft wooly coat, or an excessively long coat is to be severely penalized.

Color—The coat is liver and white, usually either liver and white spotted, liver roan, liver and white spotted with ticking and roaning or sometimes solid liver. The nose is dark brown. The head is brown, sometimes with a white blaze, the ears brown. Any black in the coat is to be severely penalized. Spotted and flesh-colored noses are undesirable and are to be penalized.

Size—Height of males should be from 24 to 26 inches at the withers, bitches smaller but not under 22 inches.

Approved February 7, 1959

In Germany there are five separate and distinct types of Deutsch Drahthaars. Of these five types, probably only three are of any numbers in the United States. Most in numerical strength are the dogs that will come under the ODIN type classification.

VERSATILITY IN THE FIELD

German Wirehaired Pointers have been used for very diversified kinds of hunting since their beginning as a breed. In Germany they are used on wild boar in this manner: the hunters are in a shooting stand, usually up in a tree, and the dogs are at the base of the tree with their trainers. The boars are flushed out of the thickets and shot by the hunters. The wounded boars will then seek the cover of the thickets. At this point, the dogs that have been trained to work as a brace are released. They follow the boar into the thickets and complete the kill. They will then—as a working team—drag the boar from the thicket into the clearing.

Another type of hunting in Germany that is uncommon to the United States is the hunting of the small roe deer and the red fox. These animals are tracked and run down by the dogs. After the kill is made, the dogs will either bay over the kill, directing the hunters to the game or they will retrieve the kill to their masters. In addition to being used on boar, roe deer, and fox, the other kinds of hunting are similar to what is seen in America.

When used for upland game birds (pheasant, partridge, woodcock, quail, or grouse), the dogs will work as close-working Pointers. They were not bred to cover the area, as do the faster-moving Pointers and Setters that are often handled from horseback. Instead, the German Wirehaired Pointer was developed to work for, and with, the hunter on foot. The dogs will work steadily around and through the densest cover. Upland game birds often head for the heavy thickets for protection when the hunters approach. The German Wirehaired Pointer has been bred especially to withstand the punishment this kind of cover can give to a bird dog. The protective, coarse, and wiry coat enables him to withstand the cuts and bruises that would cause dogs with less protection to turn back. German Wirehaired Pointers have been used for all kinds of hunting—upland game birds, rabbits, and even as a coon dog because of their tracking abilities. In addition to the upland kind of hunting, the German Wirehaired Pointer makes an excellent companion for the waterfowl hunter. The double coat (the dense, wiry outercoat and the soft, downy undercoat) affords enough warmth to enable one of the breed to stand the rigors of breaking ice which often accompanies the joys of duck hunting. I have had dogs swim up to a half mile to retrieve a downed duck. The larger males can easily cope with the problems of bringing in a downed Canadian goose. The dogs seem to have this attitude: if you want it done, they want to do it for you. This idea not only holds true in the various aspects of hunting, but in the house as well. They much prefer to be kept as a housepet than a kennel dog, and keeping them in the house in no way detracts from their hunting ability. In fact, I feel that they are better hunters when they are closer to their owner and master.

2. General Care For Home and Field

AVOIDING GUNSHYNESS

The raising and conditioning of a hunting dog does differ from the care of a housepet. From early puppyhood, future hunting dogs should become accustomed to "noise." I have found that in raising puppies, beginning with the first feedings when they are being weaned, the job of accustoming them to noise begins. Initially the food pans are pounded with a spoon or some other object. What does this noise routine accomplish? First, it links something that is pleasant to them, in this case food, with loud noises. As time progresses (and the time is usually quite short), the puppies will run to the front of their pen when they hear the noise, bounding happily about, expecting

Ch. Oldmill Flint (left) with his daughter Ch. Oldmill Flower. They are shown in wins under judge Virgil Johnson at the Genessee County Kennel Club. Flint is owned by Dr. U. D. Mostosky and handled by Barbara Humphries; Flower is owned by the author and handled by Dick Cooper.

The Danish import, Surhaves Tell. This stylish, birdy animal is present in the pedigrees of many German Wirehairs in the United States and is the cornerstone of the author's Oldmill Kennels.

dinner. Later, if your surroundings permit, the shooting of .22 blank cartridges may be introduced instead of the pounding of a pan. Once the puppies become accustomed to the sound of the gun, the shots should be repeated several times prior to feeding. Now, just what does all of this "monkey-business" accomplish? Any puppy raised in this manner has a very small chance of ever becoming gun-shy.

CONDITIONING THE YOUNG DOG

The conditioning of the young hunting dog should start at an early age. Many pups of 8 to 10 weeks have pointed with much intensity in back-yard training sessions. An old fly rod makes an excellent tool at this stage of training. Attach about 12 to 15 feet of light nylon line to the end of the rod, and to the end of the line perhaps a wing from a pheasant (for the puppy a large feather). The pup will almost immediately chase this lure. As he approaches, flick it away, allowing it to land ahead where he can see it land. After a few times, when it flies away from him, he will come in slower, in a stalking manner . . . then . . . hey, look at that pup—he's pointing! To break up these early points, merely flick the wing away, catch it (putting it into a pocket), and that's enough for the day. Perhaps fifteen minutes a day will tire the six month old pup—the younger ones, less time. It is important that you quit *before* your dog loses interest. Simple retrieving can also be started at an early age, but be certain that when you want him to bring the object to you, he does. Providing the weather permits—a warm summer day—the retrieving can just as easily be done from the water.

Throughout the growing period, your pup should have sufficient flesh to keep the ribs and hip bones well-covered. The more exercise your dog receives, the more food he will require to keep him in condition. The dog that is used in the field should not be overweight, but on the slim side, yet not skinny. The flesh should be firm and hard.

FEEDING

The adult dog will need from three to perhaps six cupfuls of kibble daily, depending upon the amount of exercise he gets. During the hunting season, the food requirements may be double the amount fed in the off-season. Good dietary supplements in the way of a vitamin-mineral food additive are advisable to help to keep your dog in prime condition.

CLIMATIC LIMITATIONS AND HOUSING

The German Wirehaired Pointer is adaptable and has become acclimated to the hot weather found in Texas as well as the cold of Alaska and everything in between. Probably the most important thing, should the dog be kept out-of-doors, is a draft-proof dog house with proper bedding materials. If he is kept outside, the protection afforded by the coat of a Wirehaired Pointer will enable him to withstand the coldest of weather. The type of shelter I have found to be best is quite simple. It should be large enough for the dog to move around comfortably in, but small enough to contain the dog's body heat during cold weather. A porch and an entryway are other refinements that can be added to the house, or, if you are not handy with tools, there are a number of fine models available in your local pet shop. Any house should be slightly raised and have a roof the dog can sit on in wet weather. The floor, walls and roof should be insulated if the temperature reaches either extreme cold or extreme heat. It is advisable, if the dog to be housed is young (Note: puppies under six months in the house during winter, please!!), to have the exposed edges covered with metal to eliminate chewing problems. A good winter bedding is clean wheat straw—this will provide ample warmth. One of the better summer bedding materials is cedar shavings. The shavings will give a good, clean odor to the dog and it helps to eliminate fleas as well.

LEADS AND COLLARS

The right collar and lead are most important in the management of your German Wirehaired Pointer, indeed more important than most people tend to think.

Most owners who use their dogs in the field prefer flat leather, buckle type collars. This is the sort most frequently seen on many sporting breeds. The owner who plans to show his dog, as well as shoot over him, may choose to have his dog wear a rolled leather collar, as this one tends to be easier on

208-375-2974

The best field dogs are those that have had thoughtful training from an early age. When they are trained early to enjoy their work they will always be better shooting companions.

the coat. It is not a good idea to let the dog wear a choke collar, particularly if he is being used in the hunting field. Too many dogs have been strangled to death when the ring in their choke collars became caught on a bush, fence-post or something of similar nature, and the dog was not found until it was too late to help him.

Regardless of the collar the dog wears, he should have an identification tag on it at all times.

The lead used for a German Wirehaired Pointer is usually either of canvas webbing or of a good grade of leather. Needless to say, both should be strong and should be comfortable for the owner's hand. The lead should also be fitted with a strong bolt or seeing eye snap. The right types of leads can be seen at your pet shop.

EXERCISING THE HUNTING DOG

The conditioning of the hunting dog, like that of any athlete, should be done gradually and carefully. Start the conditioning with exercise periods of perhaps fifteen minutes a day, and gradually increase to perhaps an hour. Long or extended running sessions at first will knock off excess weight too quickly, and will be too hard on your dog. Increase the amount of time and distance your dog is to run gradually. A regular schedule should be entered into perhaps a month or so before hunting season opens, in order to properly condition your dog for the rigorous physical activity that lies ahead. These running sessions can be alternated with back-yard sessions to sharpen up the pointing and retrieving as well.

3. Grooming and Coat Care

INTRODUCTION

The care and grooming of a German Wirehaired Pointer will vary greatly depending upon the type of coat the particular dog has. Those coats which are fairly short will require very little work, while those dogs with longer coats will require a great deal of care to maintain the proper condition and texture. All of the dogs, whether the coat is long or short, if properly cared for will shed very little. In the event that there is shedding, this is a sign that the dog is long overdue for a grooming session.

EQUIPMENT

The equipment that is required for grooming is very simple: most important is a good metal comb, with perhaps twenty teeth to the inch (fine). The fine-tooth comb will come in very handy to remove the dead undercoat which should shed out in warm weather. The same comb will also remove the dead outercoat. Another tool that can be used to remove the dead undercoat is a hound glove with a wire brush built into the palm.

TRIMMING

Care of the longer-coated dogs requires a great deal more time, skill, and know-how to properly remove dead hair than in the relatively shorter-coated dog. In cases where the body hair is two inches in length or more, removal of dead hair is difficult. Dead hair in this type of coat is more noticeable, as it tends to tuft, and when pulled gently with the fingers is easily removed. The coat at this time will also feel soft to the touch, and will not have the desired wiry texture. Once this soft-dead-hair condition is reached, it is best to use a stripping knife and do a thorough job of picking the old coat. Regular removal of the dead hair will result in a coat that will have a natural gloss and sheen to it.

The stripping knife should be used in this manner: hold the handle of the knife in the palm of your hand so the blade is toward your thumb, with the serrated edge away from your fingers. The blade is then between your fingers and thumb. Work your thumb against the grain of the hair in an easy manner; when a small amount of hair lies between your thumb and the blade of the knife, press the blade against your thumb, and with a pulling motion remove the hair. The serrated edge of the knife should be *dull*, never sharp. This same

Ch. Oldmill Cinnabar, owned by Erik Bergishagen is shown scoring winners enroute to the title of champion under the late Dr. A. A. Mitten at the Stone City Kennel Club. Cinnabar is being handled by Robert Schmitz.

procedure may be used, if necessary, to keep the top of the head, cheeks, and neck of the dog smooth and flat-lying. Removal of any hair from between the eyes will make the eyebrows clear and distinct over each eye. If the eyebrows should become too long, trim them with a pair of scissors to sharpen the appearance. The eyebrows, if trimmed, should be short towards the outside of the head and longer at the stop (between the eyes, above the nose).

The hair on the body should be flat-lying, and should not hide the body outline. The hair on the legs is short, except for feathering on the back sides of the front legs. Excessive hair on the underside of the tail should be removed to eliminate any feather. Any long hair between the toes or around the pads of the feet should be trimmed. Removal of this hair will also bring less mud into the house on a rainy day. In general, the dog should always appear neat and trim, never ragged.

GROOMING ROUTINE

A regular plan of grooming should be followed, perhaps monthly. Start with the head, working with the grain of the hair, either with the comb or glove; work down the chest, along the sides, and down the legs. Any feathering around the feet or under the tail should be removed with a pair of scissors. The claws should be kept short, so as not to cause the dog to lose the arch in his toes. Short claws will not be torn in the field, as will longer ones.

BATHING

Although the double coat of the German Wirehaired Pointer is designed to shed mud and dirt, there may be times when a bath is needed. Frequent bathing should be avoided, but occasional baths are beneficial and the owner should know how to do this job correctly.

When bathing a dog, always use a shampoo product specifically designed

Ch. Mueller's Schnitzel, a typical male, in a best of breed win under judge Newton L. Compere, handler Kurt Mueller.

Ch. Oldmill's Valentino, owned by J. P. Hutchins. A stylish showman, he is shown finishing to his championship at the Battle Creek Kennel Club under judge Kenneth Given, handler Dick Cooper.

for dogs. Human hair products are usually far too harsh for canine skin and coat.

Stand the dog in an ordinary bathtub and wet him thoroughly with a shower spray, using water a little hotter than lukewarm. Starting behind the ears, work up a thick lather all over the body. Save the head for last and wash it with a small cloth.

When rinsing, start with the head and be sure to remove every trace of lather. Any lather left in the coat will result in dullness and dandruff. After you have rinsed the dog completely, determine whether or not he still needs another soaping. If he does, repeat the process, if not take him out of the tub and dry him vigorously with several rough turkish towels.

Do not let the dog out for several hours after the bath. It is a good plan to bathe him at night after he has had his last exercise.

4. The New Puppy

PREPARING FOR THE PUPPY'S ARRIVAL

Because at least three out of four prospective purchasers of dogs want to buy a young rather than an adult or almost adult dog, the problem of preparing for the arrival of a permanent canine house guest almost always means preparing for the arrival of a puppy. This is not to say that there is anything wrong with purchasing an adult dog; on the contrary, such a purchase has definite advantages in that it often allows freedom from housebreaking chores and rigorous feeding schedules, and these are of definite benefit to prospective purchasers who have little time to spare. Since the great majority of dog buyers, however, prefer to watch their pet grow from sprawlingly playful puppyhood to dignified maturity, buying a dog, practically speaking, means buying a puppy.

Before you get a puppy be sure that you are willing to take the responsibility of training him and caring for his physical needs. His early training is most important, as an adult dog that is a well-behaved member of the family is the end product of your early training. Remember that your new puppy knows only a life of romping with his littermates and the security of being with his mother, and that coming into your home is a new and sometimes frightening experience for him. He will adjust quickly if you are patient with him and show him what you expect of him. If there are small children in the family be sure that they do not abuse him or play roughly with him. A puppy plays hard, but he also requires frequent periods of rest. Before he comes, decide where he is to sleep and where he is to eat. If your puppy does not have a collar, find out the size he requires and buy an inexpensive one, as he will soon outgrow it. Have the proper grooming equipment on hand. Consult the person from whom you bought the puppy as to the proper food for your puppy, and learn the feeding time and amount that he eats a day. Buy him some toys—usually the breeder will give you some particular toy or toys which he has cherished as a puppy to add to his new ones and to make him less homesick. Get everything you need from your petshop *before* you bring the puppy home.

MALE OR FEMALE?

Before buying your puppy you should have made a decision as to whether you want a male or a female. Unless you want to breed your pet and raise a litter of puppies, your preference as to the sex of your puppy is strictly a personal choice. Both sexes are pretty much the same in disposition and character, and both make equally good pets.

WHERE TO BUY YOUR PUPPY

Although petshop owners are necessarily restricted from carrying all breeds in stock, they know the best dog breeders and are sometimes able to supply quality puppies on demand. In cases in which a petshop owner is unable to obtain a dog for you, he can still refer you to a good source, such as a reputable kennel. If your local petshop proprietor is unable to either obtain a dog for you or refer you to someone from whom you can purchase one, don't give up: there are other avenues to explore. The American Kennel Club will furnish you addresses. Additional sources of information are the various magazines devoted to the dog fancy.

SIGNS OF GOOD HEALTH

Picking out a healthy, attractive little fellow to join the family circle is a different matter from picking a show dog; it is also a great deal less complicated. Often the puppy will pick you. If he does, and it is mutual admiration at first sight, he is the best puppy for you. At a reliable kennel or petshop the owner will be glad to answer your questions and to point out the difference between pet and show-quality puppies. Trust your eyes and hands to tell if the puppies are sound in body and temperament. Ears and eyes should not have suspicious discharges. Legs should have strong bones; bodies should have solid muscles. Coats should be clean. Lift the hair to see if the skin is free of scales and parasites.

Temperament can vary from puppy to puppy in the same litter. There is always one puppy which will impress you by his energy and personality. He loves to show off and will fling himself all over you and his littermates, and everyone who comes to see the puppies falls in love with him. However, do not overlook the more reserved puppy. Most dogs are wary of strangers, so reserve may indicate caution, not a timid puppy. He may calmly accept your presence when he senses that all is well. Such a puppy should be a steady reliable dog when mature. In any event, never force yourself on a puppy — let him come to you. Reliable breeders and petshops will urge you to take your puppy to the veterinarian of your choice to have the puppy's health checked, and will allow you at least two days in which to have it done. It should be clearly understood whether rejection by a veterinarian for health reasons means that you have the choice of another puppy from that litter or that you get your money back.

AGE AT WHICH PUPPY SHOULD BE PURCHASED

A puppy should be at least six weeks of age before you take him home. Many breeders will not let puppies go before they are two months old. In general, the puppy you buy for show and breeding should be five or six months old. If you want a show dog, remember that not even an expert can predict with 100% accuracy what a small puppy will be when he grows up.

PAPERS

When you buy a purebred dog you should receive his American Kennel Club registration certificate (or an application form to fill out), a pedigree, and a health certificate made out by the breeder's veterinarian. The registration certificate is the official A.K.C. paper. If the puppy was named and registered by his breeder you will want to complete the transfer and send it, with the fee, to the American Kennel Club. They will transfer the dog to your ownership in their records and send a new certificate to you. If you receive, instead, an application for registration, you should fill it out, choosing a name for your dog, and mail it, with the fee, to the A.K.C.

The pedigree is a chart showing your puppy's ancestry and is not a part of his official papers. The health certificate will tell what shots have been given and when the next ones are due. Your veterinarian will be appreciative of this information, and will continue with the same series of shots if they have not been completed. The health certificate will also give the dates on which the puppy has been wormed. Ask your veterinarian whether rabies shots are required in your locality. Most breeders will give you food for a few days along with instructions for feeding so that your puppy will have the same diet he is accustomed to until you can buy a supply at your petshop.

THE PUPPY'S FIRST NIGHT WITH YOU

The puppy's first night at home is likely to be disturbing to the family. Keep in mind that suddenly being away from his mother, brothers, and sisters is a new experience for him; he may be confused and frightened. If you have a special room in which you have his bed, be sure that there is nothing there with which he can harm himself. Be sure that all lamp cords are out of his reach and that there is nothing that he can tip or pull over. Check furniture that he might get stuck under or behind and objects that he might chew. If you want him to sleep in your room he probably will be quiet all night, reassured by your presence. If left in a room by himself he will cry and howl, and you will have to steel yourself to be impervious to his whining. After a few nights alone he will adjust. The first night that he is alone it is wise to put a loud-ticking alarm clock, as well as his toys, in the room with him. The alarm clock will make a comforting noise, and he will not feel that he is alone.

YOUR PUPPY'S BED

Every dog likes to have a place that is his alone. He holds nothing more sacred than his own bed whether it be a rug, dog crate, or dog bed. If you get your puppy a bed be sure to get one which discourages chewing. Also be sure that the bed is large enough to be comfortable for him when he is fully grown. Locate it away from drafts and radiators. A word might be said here in defense of the crate, which many pet owners think is cruel and confining. Given a choice, a young dog instinctively selects a secure place

Special dog feeding and watering utensils are so designed as to safeguard your pet from dangerous porcelain chips. These utensils are easy to keep clean, too.

in which to lounge, rest, or sleep. The walls and ceiling of a crate, even a wire one, answer that need. Once he regards his crate as a safe and reassuring place to stay, you will be able to leave him alone in the house.

FEEDING YOUR PUPPY

As a general rule, a puppy from weaning time (six weeks) to three months of age should have *four meals a day;* from three months to six months, *three meals;* from six months to one year, *two meals.* After a year, a dog does well on *one meal daily.* There are as many feeding schedules as there are breeders, and puppies do fine on all of them, so it is best for the new owner to follow the one given him by the breeder of his puppy. Remember that all dogs are individuals. The amount that will keep your dog in good health is right for him, not the "rule-book" amount. A feeding schedule to give you some idea of what the average puppy will eat is as follows:

Morning meal: Puppy meal with milk.

Afternoon meal: Meat mixed with puppy meal, plus a vitamin-mineral supplement.

Evening meal: Same as afternoon meal, but without a vitamin-mineral supplement.

Do not change the amounts in your puppy's diet too rapidly. If he gets diarrhea it may be that he is eating too much, so cut back on his food and when he is normal again increase his food more slowly.

There is a canned food made especially for puppies which you can buy only by a veterinarian's prescription. Some breeders use this very successfully from weaning to three months.

TRANSITIONAL DIET

Changing over to an adult program of feeding is not difficult. Very often the puppy will change himself; that is, he will refuse to eat some of his meals. He adjusts to his one meal (or two meals) a day without any trouble at all.

BREAKING TO COLLAR AND LEASH

Puppies are usually broken to a collar before you bring them home, but even if yours has never worn one it is a simple matter to get him used to it. Put a loose collar on him for a few hours at a time. At first he may scratch at it and try to get it off, but gradually he will take it as a matter of course. To break him to a lead, attach his leash to his collar and let him drag it around. When he becomes used to it pick it up and gently pull him in the direction you want him to go. He will think it is a game, and with a bit of patience on your part he will allow himself to be led.

DISCIPLINING YOUR PUPPY

The way to have a well-mannered adult dog is to give him firm basic training while he is a puppy. When you say *"No"* you must mean *"No."* Your dog will respect you only if you are firm. A six- to eight-weeks-old puppy is old enough to understand what *"No"* means. The first time you see your puppy doing something he shouldn't be doing, chewing something he shouldn't chew, or wandering in a forbidden area, it's time to teach him. Shout, *"No."* Puppies do not like loud noises, and your misbehaving pet will readily connect the word with something unpleasant. Usually a firm *"No"* in a disapproving tone of voice is enough to correct your dog, but occasionally you get a puppy that requires a firmer hand, especially as he grows older. In this case hold your puppy firmly and slap him gently across the hindquarters. If this seems cruel, you should realize that no dog resents being disciplined if he is caught in the act of doing something wrong, and your puppy will be intelligent enough to know what the slap was for.

After you have slapped him and you can see that he has learned his lesson, call him to you and talk to him in a pleasant tone of voice — praise him for coming to you. This sounds contradictory, but it works with a puppy. He immediately forgives you, practically tells you that it was his fault and that he deserved his punishment, and promises that it will not happen again. This form of discipline works best and may be used for all misbehaviors.

Never punish your puppy by chasing him around, making occasional swipes with a rolled-up newspaper; punish him only when you have a firm hold on him. Above all, never punish your dog after having called him to you. He must learn to associate coming to you with something pleasant.

HOUSEBREAKING

While housebreaking your puppy do not let him have the run of the house. If you do you will find that he will pick out his own bathroom, which may be in your bedroom or in the middle of the living room rug. Keep him confined to a small area where you can watch him, and you will be able to train him much more easily and speedily. A puppy does not want to dirty his bed, but he does need to be taught where he should go. Spread papers over his living quarters, then watch him carefully. When you notice him starting to whimper, sniff the floor, or run agitatedly in little circles, rush him to the place that you want to serve as his relief area and gently hold him there until he relieves himself. Then praise him lavishly. When you remove the soiled papers, leave a small damp piece so that the puppy's sense of smell will lead him back there next time. If he makes a mistake, wash the area at once with warm water, followed by a rinse with water and vinegar or sudsy ammonia. This will kill the odor and prevent discoloration. It shouldn't take more than a few days for him to get the idea of using newspapers. When he becomes fairly consistent, reduce the area of paper to a few sheets in a corner. As soon as you think he has the idea fixed in his mind, you can let him roam around the house a bit, but keep an eye on him. It might be best to keep him on leash the first few days so that you can rush him back to his paper at any signs of an approaching accident.

The normal healthy puppy will want to relieve himself when he wakes up in the morning, after each feeding, and after strenuous exercise. During early puppyhood any excitement, such as the return home of a member of the family or the approach of a visitor, may result in floor-wetting, but that phase should pass in a few weeks. Keep in mind that you can't expect too much from your puppy until he is about five months old. Before that, his muscles and digestive system just aren't under his control.

OUTDOOR HOUSEBREAKING

You can begin outdoor training on leash even while you are paper-training your puppy. First thing in the morning take him outdoors (to the curb, if you are in the city) and walk him back and forth in a small area until he relieves himself. He will probably make a puddle and then walk around, uncertain of what is expected of him. You can try standing him over a newspaper, which may give him the idea. Some dog trainers use glycerine suppositories at this point for fast action. Praise your dog every time taking him outside brings results, and he will get the idea. You'll find, when you begin the outdoor training, that the male puppy usually requires a longer walk than the female. Both male and female puppies will squat. It isn't until he is older that the male dog will begin to lift his leg. If you hate to give up your sleep, you can train your puppy to go outdoors during the day and use the paper at night.

5. Training

WHEN TO START TRAINING

You should never begin SERIOUS obedience training before your dog is seven or eight months old. (Some animal psychologists state that puppies can begin training when seven weeks old, if certain techniques are followed. These techniques, however, are still experimental and should be left to the professional trainer to prove their worth.) While your dog is still in his early puppyhood, concentrate on winning his confidence so he will love and admire you. This will make his training easier, since he will do anything to please you. Basic training can be started at the age of three or four months. He should be taught to walk nicely on a leash, sit and lie down on command, and come when he is called.

YOUR PART IN TRAINING

You must patiently demonstrate to your dog what each word of command means. Guide him with your hands and the training leash, reassuring him with your voice, through whatever routine you are teaching him. Repeat the word associated with the act. Demonstrate again and again to give the dog a chance to make the connection in his mind.

Once he begins to get the idea, use the word of command without any physical guidance. Drill him. When he makes mistakes, correct him, kindly at first, more severely as his training progresses. Try not to lose your patience or become irritated, and never slap him with your hand or the leash during the training session. Withholding praise or rebuking him will make him feel bad enough.

When he does what you want, praise him lavishly with words and with pats. Don't continually reward with dog candy or treats in training. The dog that gets into the habit of performing for a treat will seldom be fully dependable when he can't smell or see one in the offing. When he carries out a command, even though his performance is slow or sloppy, praise him and he will perform more readily the next time.

THE TRAINING VOICE

When you start training your dog, use your training voice, giving commands in a firm, clear tone. Once you give a command, persist until it is obeyed, even if you have to pull the dog to obey you. He must learn that training is different from playing, that a command once given must be obeyed no matter what distractions are present. Remember that the tone and pitch of your voice, not loudness, are the qualities that will influence your dog most.

Be consistent in the use of words during training. Confine your commands to as few words as possible and never change them. It is best for only one person to carry on the dog's training, because different people will use different words and tactics that will confuse your dog. The dog who hears *"come," "get over here," "hurry up," "here, Rex,"* and other commands when he is wanted will become totally confused.

TRAINING LESSONS

Training is hard on the dog — and on the trainer. A young dog just cannot take more than ten minutes of training at a stretch, so limit the length of your first lessons. Then you can gradually increase the length of time to about thirty minutes. You'll find that you too will tend to become impatient when you stretch out a training lesson. If you find yourself losing your temper, stop and resume the lesson at another time. Before and after each lesson have a play period, but don't play during a training session. Even the youngest dog soon learns that schooling is a serious matter; fun comes afterward.

Don't spend too much time on one phase of the training, or the dog will become bored. Always try to end a lesson on a pleasant note. Actually, in nine cases out of ten, if your dog isn't doing what you want it's because you're not getting the idea over to him properly.

YOUR TRAINING EQUIPMENT AND ITS USE

The leash is more properly called the lead, so we'll use that term here. The best leads for training are the six-foot webbed-cloth leads, usually olive-drab in color, and the six-foot leather lead. Fancier leads are available and may be used if desired.

You'll need a metal-link collar, called a choke chain, consisting of a metal chain with rings on each end. Even though the name may sound frightening, it won't hurt your dog, and it is an absolute MUST in training. There is a right and a wrong way to put the training collar on. It should go around the dog's neck so that you can attach the lead to the ring at the end of the chain which passes OVER, not under his neck. It is most important that the collar is put on properly so it will tighten when the lead is pulled and ease when you relax your grip.

The correct way to hold the lead is also very important, as the collar should have some slack in it, at all times, except when correcting. Holding the loop in your right hand, extend your arm out to the side, even with your shoulder. With your left hand, grasp the lead as close as possible to the collar, without making it tight. The remaining portion of the lead can be made into a loop which is held in the right hand. Keep this arm close to your body. Most corrections will be made with the left hand by giving the lead a jerk in the direction you want the dog to go. The dog that pulls and forges ahead can be corrected by a steady pull on the lead.

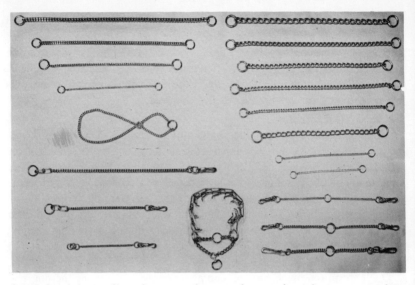

Special training collars for your dog can be purchased at your petshop.

HEELING

"*Heeling*" in dog language means having your dog walk alongside you on your left side, close to your leg, on lead or off. With patience and effort you can train your dog to walk with you even on a crowded street or in the presence of other dogs.

Now that you have learned the correct way to put on your dog's collar and how to hold the lead, you are ready to start with his first lesson in heeling. Put the dog at your left side, sitting. Using the dog's name and the command "*Heel*," start forward on your LEFT foot, giving a tug on the lead to get the dog started. Always use the dog's name first, followed by the command, such as "*Rex, heel.*" Saying his name will help get his attention and will let him know that you are about to give a command.

Walk briskly, with even steps, going around in a large circle, square, or straight line. While walking, make sure that your dog stays on the left side and close to your leg. If he lags behind, give several tugs on the lead to get him up to you, then praise him for doing well. If he forges ahead or swings wide, stop and jerk the lead sharply and bring him back to the proper position. Always repeat the command when correcting, and praise him when he does well. If your dog continues to pull or lag behind, either your corrections are not severe enough or your timing between correction and praise is off. Do this exercise for only five minutes at first, gradually lengthening it to fifteen, or even half an hour.

To keep your dog's attention, talk to him as you keep him in place. You can also do a series of fast about-turns, giving the lead a jerk as you turn. He will gradually learn that he must pay attention or be jerked to your side. You can vary the routine by changing speeds, doing turns, figure-eights, and by zig-zagging across the training area.

"HEEL" MEANS "SIT," TOO

To the dog, the command "*Heel*" will also mean that he has to sit in the heel position at your left side when you stop walking — with no additional command from you. As you practice heeling, make him sit whenever you stop, at first using the word "*Sit,*" then with no command at all. He'll soon get the idea and sit down when you stop and wait for the command "*Heel*" to start walking again.

TRAINING TO SIT

Training your dog to sit should be fairly easy. Stand him on your left side, holding the lead fairly short, and command him to "*Sit.*" As you give the verbal command, pull up slightly with the lead and push his hindquarters down. Do not let him lie down or stand up. Keep him in a sitting position for a moment, then release the pressure on the lead and praise him. Constantly repeat the command as you hold him in a sitting position, thus fitting the word to the action in his mind. After a while he will begin to get the idea and will sit without your having to push his hindquarters down. When he reaches that stage, insist that he sit on command. If he is slow to obey, slap his hindquarters with your hand to get him down fast. *DO NOT HIT HIM HARD!* Teach him to sit on command facing you as well as when he is at your side. When he begins sitting on command with the lead on, try it with the lead off.

THE "LIE DOWN"

The object of this is to get the dog to lie down either on the verbal command "*Down*" or when you give him the hand signal, your hand raised in front of you, palm down. This is one of the most important parts of training. A well-trained dog will drop on command and stay down whatever the temptation: cat-chasing, car-chasing, or another dog across the street.

Don't start training to lie down until the dog is almost letter-perfect in sitting on command. Then place the dog in a sit, and kneel before him. With both hands, reach forward to his legs and take one front leg in each hand, thumbs up, and holding just below his elbows. Lift his legs slightly off the ground and pull them somewhat out in front of him. Simultaneously, give the command "*Down*" and lower his front legs to the ground.

Hold the dog down and stroke him to let him know that staying down is what you want him to do. This method is far better than forcing a young dog down. Using force can cause him to become very frightened and he will begin to dislike any training. Always talk to your dog and let him know that you are very pleased with him, and soon you will find that you have a happy working dog.

After he begins to get the idea, slide the lead under your left foot and give the command "*Down.*" At the same time, pull the lead. This will help get the dog down. Meanwhile, raise your hand in the down signal. Don't expect to accomplish all this in one session. Be patient and work with the dog. He'll cooperate if you show him just what you expect him to do.

THE "STAY"

The next step is to train your dog to stay either in a "*Sit*" or "*Down*" position. Sit him at your side. Give the command "*Stay,*" but be careful not to use his name with this command, because hearing his name may lead him to think that some action is expected of him. If he begins to move, repeat "*Stay*" firmly and hold him down in the sit. Constantly repeat the word "*Stay*" to fix the meaning of that command in his mind. After he has learned to stay for a short time, gradually increase the length of his stay. The hand signal for the stay is a downward sweep of your hand toward the dog's nose, with the palm facing him. While he is sitting, walk around him and stand in front of him. Hold the lead at first; later, drop the lead on the ground in front of him and keep him sitting. If he bolts, scold him and place him back in the same position, repeating the command and all the exercise.

Use some word such as "*Okay*" or "*Up*" to let him know when he can get up, and praise him well for a good performance. As this practice continues, walk farther and farther away from him. Later, try sitting him, giving the command to stay, and then walk out of sight, first for a few seconds, then for longer periods. A well-trained dog should stay where you put him without moving until you come and release him.

Similarly, practice having him stay in the down position, first with you near him, later when you step out of sight.

THE "COME" ON COMMAND

You can train your dog to come when you call him, if you begin when he is young. At first, work with him on lead. Sit the dog, then back away the length of the lead and call him, putting into your voice as much coaxing affection as possible. Give an easy tug on the lead to get him started. When he does come, make a big fuss over him; it might help at this point to give him a small piece of dog candy or food as a reward. He should get the idea soon. You can also move away from him the full length of the lead and call to him something like "*Rex, come,*" then run backward a few steps and stop, making him sit directly in front of you.

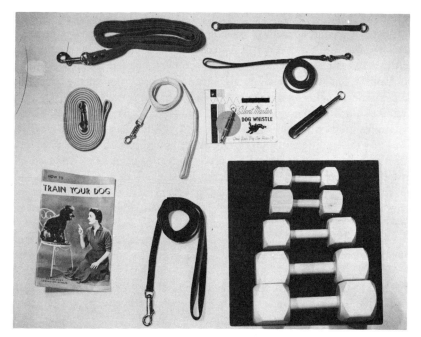

Visit your petshop for all of the training equipment you will need to make your pet a better canine citizen.

Don't be too eager to practice coming on command off lead. Wait until you are certain that you have the dog under perfect control before you try calling him when he's free. Once he gets the idea that he can disobey a command and get away with it, your training program will suffer a serious setback. Keep in mind that your dog's life may depend on his immediate response to a command to come when he is called. If he disobeys off lead, put the lead back on and correct him severely with jerks of the lead.

TEACHING TO COME TO HEEL

The object of this is for you to stand still, say *"Heel,"* and have your dog come right over to you and sit by your left knee in the heel position. If your dog has been trained to sit without command every time you stop, he's ready for this step.

Sit him in front of and facing you and step back one step. Moving only your left foot, pull the dog behind you, then step forward and pull him around until he is in a heel position. You can also have the dog go around by passing the lead behind your back. Use your left heel to straighten him out if he begins to sit behind you or crookedly. This may take a little work, but he will get the idea if you show him just what you want.

THE "STAND"

Your dog should be trained to stand in one spot without moving his feet, and he should allow a stranger to run his hand over his body and legs without showing any resentment or fear. Employ the same method you used in training him to stay on the sit and down. While walking, place your left hand out, palm toward his nose, and command him to stay. His first impulse will be to sit, so be prepared to stop him by placing your hand under his body, near his hindquarters, and holding him until he gets the idea that this is different from the command to sit. Praise him for standing, then walk to the end of the lead. Correct him strongly if he starts to move. Have a stranger approach him and run his hands over the dog's back and down his legs. Keep him standing until you come back to him. Walk around him from his left side, come to the heel position, and make sure that he does not sit until you command him to.

This is a very valuable exercise. If you plan to show your dog he will have learned to stand in a show pose and will allow the judge to examine him.

TRAINING SCHOOLS AND CLASSES

There are dog-training classes in all parts of the country, some sponsored by the local humane society.

If you feel that you lack the time or the skill to train your dog yourself, there are professional dog trainers who will do it for you, but basically dog training is a matter of training YOU and your dog to work together as a team, and if you don't do it yourself you will miss a lot of fun. Don't give up after trying unsuccessfully for a short time. Try a little harder and you and your dog will be able to work things out.

ADVANCED TRAINING AND OBEDIENCE TRIALS

Once you begin training your dog and you see how well he does, you'll probably be bitten by the "obedience bug" — the desire to enter him in obedience trials held under American Kennel Club auspices.

The A.K.C. obedience trials are divided into three classes: Novice, Open, and Utility.

In the Novice Class, the dog will be judged on the following basis:

TEST	MAXIMUM SCORE
Heel on lead	35
Stand for examination	30
Heel free — off lead	45
Recall (come on command)	30
One-minute sit (handler in ring)	30
Three-minute down (handler in ring)	30
Maximum total score	200

If the dog "qualifies" in three shows by earning at least 50% of the points for each test, with a total of at least 170 for the trial, he has earned the Companion Dog degree and the letters C.D. (Companion Dog) are entered after his name in the A.K.C. records.

After the dog has qualified as a C.D., he is eligible to enter the Open Class competition, where he will be judged on this basis:

TEST	MAXIMUM SCORE
Heel free	40
Drop on Recall	30
Retrieve (wooden dumbbell) on flat	25
Retrieve over obstacle (hurdle)	35
Broad jump	20
Three-minute sit (handler out of ring)	25
Five-minute down (handler out of ring)	25
Maximum total score	200

Again he must qualify in three shows for the C.D.X. (Companion Dog Excellent) title and then is eligible for the Utility Class, where he can earn the Utility Dog (U.D.) degree in these rugged tests:

TEST	MAXIMUM SCORE
Scent discrimination (picking up article handled by master from group) Article 1	20
Scent discrimination Article 2	20
Scent discrimination Article 3	20
Seek back (picking up an article dropped by handler)	30
Signal exercise (heeling, etc., on hand signal)	35
Directed jumping (over hurdle and bar jump)	40
Group examination	35
Maximum total score	200

For more complete information about these obedience trials, write for the American Kennel Club's *Regulations and Standards for Obedience Trials*. Dogs that are disqualified from breed shows because of alteration or physical defects are eligible to compete in these trials. Besides the formal A.K.C. obedience trials, there are informal "match" shows in which dogs compete for ribbons and inexpensive trophies. These shows are run by many local fanciers' dog clubs and by all-breed obedience clubs. In many localities the humane society and other groups conduct their own obedience shows. Your local petshop or kennel can keep you informed about such shows in your vicinity, and you will find them listed in the different dog magazines or in the pet column of your local newspaper.

6. Breeding

THE QUESTION OF SPAYING

If you feel that you will never want to raise a litter of purebred puppies, and if you do not wish to risk the possibility of an undesirable mating and surplus mongrel puppies inevitably destined for execution at the local pound, you may want to have your female spayed. Spaying is generally best performed after the female has passed her first heat and before her first birthday: this allows the female to attain the normal female characteristics, while still being young enough to avoid the possible complications encountered when an older female is spayed. A spayed female will remain a healthy, lively pet. You often hear that an altered female will become very fat. However, if you cut down on her food intake, she will not gain weight.

On the other hand, if you wish to show your dog (altered females are disqualified) or enjoy the excitement and feeling of accomplishment of breeding and raising a litter of puppies, particularly in your breed and from your pet, then definitely do not spay.

Male dogs, unlike tomcats, are almost never altered (castrated).

SEXUAL PHYSIOLOGY

Females usually reach sexual maturity (indicated by the first heat cycle, or season) at eight or nine months of age, but sexual maturity may occur as early as six months or as late as thirteen months of age. The average heat cycle (estrus period) lasts for twenty or twenty-one days, and occurs approximately every six months. For about five days immediately preceding the heat period, the female generally displays restlessness and an increased appetite. The vulva, or external genitals, begin to swell. The discharge, which is bright red at the onset and gradually becomes pale pink to straw in color, increases in quantity for several days and then slowly subsides, finally ceasing altogether. The vaginal discharge is subject to much variation: in some bitches it is quite heavy, in others it may never appear, and in some it may be so slight as to go unnoticed.

About eight or nine days after the first appearance of the discharge, the female becomes very playful with other dogs, but will not allow a mating to take place. Anywhere from the tenth or eleventh day, when the discharge has virtually ended and the vulva has softened, to the seventeenth or eighteenth day, the female will accept males and be able to conceive. Many biologists apply the term "heat" only to this receptive phase rather than to the whole estrus, as is commonly done by dog fanciers.

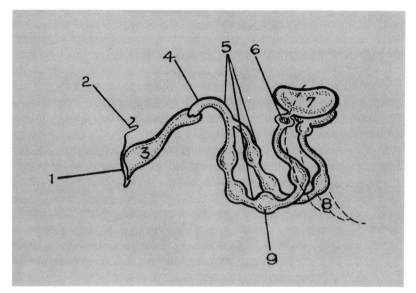

The reproduction system of the bitch: 1, vulva; 2, anus; 3, vagina; 4, cervix; 5, uterus; 6, ovary; 7, kidneys; 8, ribs; 9, fetal lump.

The ova (egg cells) from the female's ovaries are discharged into the oviduct toward the close of the acceptance phase, usually from the sixteenth to eighteenth day. From the eighteenth day until the end of the cycle, the female is still attractive to males, but she will repulse their advances. The entire estrus, however, may be quite variable: in some females vaginal bleeding ends and mating begins on the fourth day; in others, the discharge may continue throughout the entire cycle and the female will not accept males until the seventeenth day or even later.

The male dog — simply referred to by fanciers as the "dog," in contrast to the female, which is referred to as the "bitch" — upon reaching sexual maturity, usually at about six to eight months, is able, like other domesticated mammals, to breed at any time throughout the year.

The testes, the sperm-producing organs of the male, descend from the body cavity into the scrotum at birth. The condition of *cryptorchidism* refers to the retention of one or both testes within the body cavity. A testicle retained within the body cavity is in an environment too hot for it to function normally. A retained testicle may also become cancerous. If only one testicle descends, the dog is known as a *monorchid;* if neither descends, the dog is known as an *anorchid* (dog fanciers, however, refer to a dog with the latter condition as a cryptorchid). A monorchid dog is a fertile animal; an anorchid is sterile.

The male dog's penis has a bulbous enlargement at its base and, in addition, like the penis of a number of other mammals, contains a bone. When mating occurs, pressure on the penis causes a reflex action that fills the bulb with blood, swelling it to about five times its normal size within the female. This locks, or ties, the two animals together. After ejaculation, the animals usually remain tied for fifteen to thirty minutes, but they may separate very quickly or remain together an hour or more, depending on the length of time it takes for the blood to drain from the bulb.

CARE OF THE FEMALE IN ESTRUS

If you have a dog-proof run within your yard, it will be safe to leave your female in season there; if you don't have such a run, she should be shut indoors. Don't leave her alone outside even for a minute; she should be exercised only on lead. If you want to prevent the neighborhood dogs from congregating around your doorstep, as they inevitably will as soon as they discover that your female is in season, take her some distance from the house before you let her relieve herself. Take her in your car to a park or field for a chance to "stretch" her legs (always on lead of course). Keep watch for male dogs, and if one approaches take the female back to the car. After the three weeks are up you can let her out as before with no worry that she can have puppies until her next season.

Some owners find it simpler to board their female at a kennel until her season is over. However, it really is not difficult to watch your female at home. There are various products on the market which are useful at this time. Although the female in season keeps herself quite clean, sometimes she unavoidably stains furniture or rugs. You can buy sanitary belts made especially for dogs at your petshop. Consult your veterinarian for information on pills to be taken to check odor during this period. There also is a pill that prevents the female from coming in season for extended periods, and there are many different types of liquids, powders, and sprays of varying efficiency used to keep male dogs away. However, the one safe rule (whatever products you use) is: keep your bitch away from dogs that could mount her.

SHOULD YOU BREED YOUR MALE?

As with every question, whether or not to use a male dog as a stud has two sides. The arguments for and against using a dog as a stud are often very close to the ridiculous. A classic example would be the tale that once you use a dog as a stud he will lose his value as a show dog or any one of the other functions a dog may have. A sound rule may well be: *if you have a stud who has proven his worth at the shows, place his services out for hire, if only for the betterment of the breed; if your dog is not of show quality, do not use him as a stud.*

Top champion studs can bring their owners many dollars in breeding revenue. If the stud is as good as you feel he is, his services will soon be in great demand. Using a dog as a stud will not lower his value in other functions in any way. Many breeders will permit a male dog to breed an experienced female once, when about a year old, and then they begin to show their stud until he has gained his conformation championship. He is then placed out for hire through advertising in the various bulletins, journals, and show catalogs, and through the stud registers maintained by many pet-shops.

SHOULD YOU BREED YOUR FEMALE?

If you are an amateur and decide to breed your female it would be wise to talk with a breeder and find out all that breeding and caring for puppies entails. You must be prepared to assume the responsibility of caring for the mother through her pregnancy and for the puppies until they are of saleable age. Raising a litter of puppies can be a rewarding experience, but it means work as well as fun, and there is no guarantee of financial profit. As the puppies grow older and require more room and care, the amateur breeder, in desperation, often sells the puppies for much less than they are worth; sometimes he has to give them away. If the cost of keeping the puppies will drain your finances, think twice.

If you have given careful consideration to all these things and still want to breed your female, remember that there is some preparation necessary before taking this step.

WHEN TO BREED

It is usually best to breed in the second or third season. Consider when the puppies will be born and whether their birth and later care will interfere with your work or vacation plans. Gestation period is approximately fifty-eight to sixty-three days. Allow enough time to select the right stud for her. Don't be in a position of having to settle for any available male if she comes into season sooner than expected. Your female will probably be ready to breed twelve days after the first colored discharge. You can usually make arrangements to board her with the owner of the male for a few days to insure her being there at the proper time, or you can take her to be mated and bring her home the same day. If she still appears receptive she may be bred again a day or two later. Some females never show signs of willingness, so it helps to have the experience of a breeder. The second day after the discharge changes color is the proper time; she may be bred for about three days following. For an additional week or so she may have some discharge and attract other dogs by her odor, but she can seldom be bred at this time.

HOW TO SELECT A STUD

Choose a mate for your female with an eye to countering her deficiencies. If possible, both male and female should have several ancestors in common within the last two or three generations, as such combinations generally "click" best. The male should have a good show record himself or be the sire of champions. The owner of the stud usually charges a fee for the use of the dog. The fee varies. Payment of a fee does not guarantee a litter, but it does generally confer the right to breed your female again to the stud if she does not have puppies the first time. In some cases the owner of the stud will agree to take a choice puppy in place of a stud fee. You and the owner of the stud should settle all details beforehand, including such questions as what age the puppies should reach before the stud's owner can make his choice, what disposition is made of a single surviving puppy under an agreement by which the stud owner has pick of the litter, and so on. In all cases it is best that the agreement entered into by bitch owner and stud owner be in the form of a written contract.

It is customary for the female to be sent to the male; if the stud dog of your choice lives any distance you will have to make arrangements to have your female shipped to him. The quickest way is by air, and if you call your nearest airport the airline people will give you information as to the best and fastest flight. Some airlines furnish their own crates for shipping, whereas others require that you furnish your own. The owner of the stud will make the arrangements for shipping the female back to you. You have to pay all shipping charges.

PREPARATION FOR BREEDING

Before you breed your female, make sure she is in good health. She should be neither too thin nor too fat. Skin diseases must be cured before breeding; a bitch with skin diseases can pass them on to her puppies. If she has worms she should be wormed before being bred, or within three weeks afterward. It is a good idea to have your veterinarian give her a booster shot for distemper and hepatitis before the puppies are born. This will increase the immunity the puppies receive during their early, most vulnerable period. Choose a dependable veterinarian and rely on him if there is an emergency when your female whelps.

HOW OFTEN SHOULD YOU BREED YOUR FEMALE?

Do not breed your bitch after she reaches six years of age. If you wish to breed her several times while she is young, it is wise to breed her only once a year. In other words, breed her, skip a season, and then breed her again. This will allow her to gain back her full strength between whelpings.

THE IMPORTANCE AND APPLICATION OF GENETICS

Any person attempting to breed dogs should have a basic understanding of the transmission of traits, or characteristics, from the parents to the offspring and some familiarity with the more widely used genetic terms that he will probably encounter. A knowledge of the fundamental mechanics of genetics enables a breeder to better comprehend the passing, complementing, and covering of both good points and faults from generation to generation. It enables him to make a more judicial and scientific decision in selecting potential mates.

Inheritance, fundamentally, is due to the existence of microscopic units, known as *GENES,* present in the cells of all individuals. Genes somehow control the biochemical reactions that occur within the embryo or adult organism. This control results in changing or guiding the development of the organism's characteristics. A "string" of attached genes is known as a *CHROMOSOME.* With a few important exceptions, every chromosome has a partner chromosome carrying a duplicate or equivalent set of genes. Each gene, therefore, has a partner gene, known as an *ALLELE.* The number of different pairs of chromosomes present in the cells of the organism varies with the type of organism: a certain parasitic worm has only one pair, a certain fruit fly has four different pairs, man has 23 different pairs, and your dog has 39 different pairs per cell. Because each chromosome may have many hundreds of genes, a single cell of the body may contain a total of several thousand genes. Heredity is obviously a very complex matter.

In the simplest form of genetic inheritance, one particular gene and its duplicate, or allele, on the partner chromosome control a single characteristic. The presence of freckles in the human skin, for example, is believed to be due to the influence of a single pair of genes.

Each cell of the body contains the specific number of paired chromosomes characteristic of the organism. Because each type of gene is present on both chromosomes of a chromosome pair, *each type of gene is therefore present in duplicate.* The fusion of a sperm cell from the male with an egg cell from the female, as occurs in fertilization, should therefore result in offspring having a *quadruplicate number* (4) of each type of gene. Mating of these individuals would then produce progeny having an *octuplicate number* (8) of each type of gene, and so on. This, however, is normally prevented by a special process. When ordinary body cells prepare to divide to form more tissue, each pair of chromosomes duplicates itself so that there are four partner chromosomes of each kind instead of only two. When the cell divides, two of the four partners, or one pair, go into each new cell. This process, known as *MITOSIS,* insures that each new body cell contains the proper number of chromosomes. Reproductive cells (sperm cell and egg cells), however, undergo a special kind of division known as *MEIOSIS.* In meiosis, the chromosome pairs do *not* duplicate themselves, and thus when the reproductive cells reach the final dividing stage only one chromosome, or one-half of the pair, goes into each new reproductive cell. Each reproductive cell, therefore, has only half the normal number of chromosomes. These are referred to as *HAPLOID* cells, in contrast to *DIPLOID* cells, which have the full number of chromosomes.

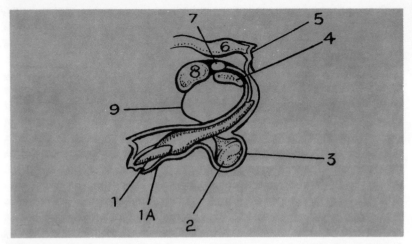

The reproductive system of a male: 1a, sheath; 1, penis; 2, testicle; 3, scrotum; 4, pelvic bone; 5, anus; 6, rectum; 7, prostate; 8, bladder; 9, vas deferens.

When the haploid sperm cell fuses with the haploid egg cell in fertilization, the resulting offspring has the normal diploid number of chromosomes.

If both partner genes, or alleles, affect the trait in an identical manner, the genes are said to be *HOMOZYGOUS*, but if one affects the character in a manner different from the other gene, or allele, the genes are said to be *HETEROZYGOUS*. For example, in the pair of genes affecting eye color in humans, if each gene of the pair produces blue eyes, the genes (and also the person carrying the genes) are said to be homozygous for blue eyes. If, however, one gene of the pair produces blue eyes, while the other gene, or allele, produces brown eyes, they are said to be heterozygous. The presence of heterozygous genes raises the question, *"Will the offspring have blue eyes or brown eyes?"* which in turn introduces another genetic principle: *DOMINANCE* and *RECESSIVENESS*.

If one gene of a pair can block the action of its partner, or allele, while still producing its own affect, that gene is said to be *dominant* over its allele. Its allele, on the other hand, is said to be recessive. In the case of heterozygous genes for eye color, the brown eye gene is dominant over the recessive blue eye gene, and the offspring therefore will have brown eyes. Much less common is the occurrence of gene pairs in which neither gene is completely dominant over the other. This, known as *INCOMPLETE* or *PARTIAL DOMINANCE,* results in a blending of the opposing influences. In cattle, if a homozygous (pure) red bull is mated with a homozygous (pure) white cow, the calf will be roan, a blending of red and white hairs in its coat, rather than either all red or all white.

During meiosis, or division of the reproductive (sperm and egg) cells, each pair of chromosomes splits, and one-half of each pair goes into one of the two new cells. Thus, in the case of eye color genes, one new reproductive cell will get the chromosome carrying the blue eye gene, while the other new reproductive cell will get the chromosome carrying the brown eye gene, and so on for each pair of chromosomes. If an organism has only two pairs of chromosomes — called pair A, made up of chromosomes A_1 and A_2, and pair B, made up of chromosomes B_1 and B_2 — each new reproductive cell will get one chromosome from each pair, and four different combinations are possible: A_1 and B_1; A_1 and B_2; A_2 and B_1, or A_2 and B_2. If the blue eye gene is on A_1, the brown eye gene on A_2, the gene for curly hair on B_1 and the gene for straight hair on B_2, each of the above combinations will exert a different genetic effect on the offspring. This different grouping of chromosomes in the new reproductive cell as a result of meiotic cell division is known as *INDEPENDENT ASSORTMENT* and is one reason why variation occurs in the offspring. In the dog, with 39 pairs of chromosomes, the possibilities of variation through independent assortment are tremendous.

But variation does not end here. For example, if two dominant genes, such as the genes for brown eyes and dark hair, were on the same chromosome, all brown-eyed people would have dark hair. Yet in instances where such joined or *LINKED* genes do occur, the two characteristics do not always appear together in the same offspring. This is due to a process known as *CROSS-OVER* or *RECOMBINATION*. Recombination is the mutual exchange of corresponding blocks of genes between the two chromosomes in a pair. That is, during cell division, the two chromosomes may exchange their tip sections or other corresponding segments. If the segments exchanged contain the eye color genes, the brown eye gene will be transferred from the chromosome carrying the dark hair gene to the chromosome carrying the light hair gene, and then brown eyes will occur with light hair, provided that the individual is homozygous for the recessive light hair gene.

Another important source of variation is *MUTATION*. In mutation, a gene becomes altered, such as by exposure to irradiation, and exerts a different effect than it did before. Most mutations are harmful to the organism, and some may result in death. Offspring carrying mutated genes and showing the effects of these mutations are known as *MUTANTS* or *SPORTS*. Mutation also means that instead of only two alleles for eye color, such as brown and blue, there may now be three or more (gray, black, etc.) creating a much larger source for possible variation in the offspring.

Further complications in the transmission and appearance of genetic traits are the phenomena known as *EPISTASIS* and *PLEIOTROPY*. Epistasis refers to a gene exerting influence on genes other than its own allele.

In all-white red-eyed (albino) guinea pigs, for example, the gene controlling intensity of color is epistatic to any other color gene and prevents that gene from producing its effect. Thus, even if a gene for red spots were present in the cells of the guinea pig, the color intensity gene would prevent the red spots from appearing in the guinea pig's white coat. *Pleiotropy* refers to the fact that a single gene may control a number of characteristics. In the fruit fly, for example, the gene that controls eye color may also affect the structure of certain body parts and even the lifespan of the insect.

One special pair of chromosomes is known as the sex chromosomes. In man, dog, and other mammals, these chromosomes are of two types, designated as X and Y. Under normal conditions, a mammal carrying two X-type sex chromosomes is a female, whereas a mammal carrying one X-type and one Y-type is a male. Females, therefore, have only X chromosomes and can only contribute X chromosomes to the offspring, but the male may contribute either an X or a Y.

If the male's sperm carrying an X chromosome fertilizes the female's egg cell (X), the offspring (XX) will be female; if a sperm carrying a Y chromosome fertilizes the egg (X), the offspring (XY) will be male. It is the male, therefore, that determines the sex of the offspring in mammals.

Traits controlled by genes present on the sex chromosome, and which appear in only one sex, are said to be *SEX LINKED*. If, for example, a rare recessive gene occurs on the X chromosome, it cannot exert its effect in the female because the dominant allele on the other X chromosome will counteract it. In the male, however, there is no second X chromosome, and if the Y chromosome cannot offer any countereffect, the recessive character will appear. There are also *SEX-LIMITED* characteristics: these appear primarily or solely in one sex, but the genes for these traits are not carried on the sex chromosomes. Sex-limited traits appear when genes on other chromosomes exert their effect in the proper hormonal (male or female) environment. Sex-linked and sex-limited transmission is how a trait may skip a generation, by being passed from grandfather to grandson through a mother in which the trait, though present, does not show.

In dealing with the simplest form of heredity — one gene effecting one character — there is an expected ratio of the offspring displaying the character to those who do not display it, depending upon the genetic makeup of the parents. If a parent is homozygous for a character, such as blue eyes, it makes no difference which half of the chromosome pair enters the new reproductive cell, because each chromosome carries the gene for blue eyes. If a parent is heterozygous, however, one reproductive cell will receive the brown eye gene while the other will receive the blue eye gene. If both parents are homozygous for blue eyes, all the offspring will receive two blue eye genes, and all will have blue eyes. If a parent is homozygous for blue eyes, and the other parent is homozygous for brown eyes, all the offspring will be heterozygous, receiving one brown eye gene and one blue eye gene, and because brown is dominant, all will have brown eyes. If both parents are heterozygous, both the blue eye gene and the brown eye gene from one parent have an equal likelihood of ending up with either the blue eye or the brown eye gene from the other parent. This results in a ratio of two heterozygous offspring to the one homozygous for brown eyes and one homozygous for blue eyes, giving a total genetic, or genotypic, ratio of $2:1:1$ or, as it is more commonly arranged, $1:2:1$. As the two heterozygous as well as the homozygous brown eye offspring will have brown eyes, the ratio of brown eyes to blue eyes (or phenotypic ratio) will be $3:1$.

If one parent is heterozygous and the other parent is homozygous for the recessive gene for blue eyes, half of the offspring will be homozygous for blue eyes and will have blue eyes, but the other half of the offspring will be heterozygous and have brown eyes. (Here both the genotypic and phenotypic ratio is $1:1$.)

If the homozygous parent, however, has the dominant gene (brown eyes), half of the offspring will be heterozygous and half will be homozygous, as before, but all will have brown eyes. By repeated determinations of these ratios in the offspring, geneticists are able to analyze the genetic makeup of the parents.

Before leaving heredity, it might be well to explain the difference between inbreeding, outcrossing, line breeding, and similar terms. Basically, there are only inbreeding and outbreeding. Inbreeding, however, according to its intensity, is usually divided into inbreeding proper and line breeding. Inbreeding proper is considered to be the mating of very closely related individuals, generally within the immediate family, but this is sometimes extended to include matings to first cousins and grandparents. Line breeding is the mating of more distantly related animals, that is, animals, not immediately related to each other but having a common ancestor, such as the same grandsire or great-grandsire. Outbreeding is divided into outcrossing, which is the mating of dogs from different families within the same breed, and cross-breeding, which is mating purebred dogs from different breeds.

From the foregoing discussion of genetics, it should be realized that the theory of telegony, which states that the sire of one litter can influence future litters sired by other studs, is simply not true; it is possible, however, if several males mate with a female during a single estrus cycle, that the various puppies in the litter may have different sires (but not two sires for any one puppy). It should also be realized that blood does not really enter into the transmission of inheritance, although people commonly speak of "bloodlines," "pure-blooded," etc.

7. Care of the Mother and Family

PRENATAL CARE OF THE FEMALE

You can expect the puppies nine weeks from the day of breeding, although 58 days is as common as 63. During this time the female should receive normal care and exercise. If she is overweight, don't increase her food at first; excess weight at whelping time is not good. If she is on the thin side, build her up, giving her a morning meal of cereal and egg yolk. Consult your veterinarian as to increasing her vitamins and mineral supplement. During the last weeks the puppies grow enormously, and the mother will have little room for food and less appetite. Divide her meals into smaller portions and feed her more ofen. If she loses her appetite, tempt her with meat, liver, chicken, etc.

As she grows heavier, eliminate violent exercise and jumping. Do not eliminate exercise entirely, as walking is beneficial to the female in whelp, and mild exercise will maintain her muscle tone in preparation for the birth. Weigh your female after breeding and keep a record of her weight each week thereafter. Groom your bitch daily — some females have a slight discharge during gestation, more prevalent during the last two weeks, so wash the vulva with warm water daily. Usually, by the end of the fifth week you can notice a broadening across her loins, and her breasts become firmer. By the end of the sixth week your veterinarian can tell you whether or not she is pregnant.

PREPARATION OF WHELPING QUARTERS

Prepare a whelping box at least a week before the puppies are to arrive and allow the mother-to-be to sleep there overnight or to spend some time in it during the day to become accustomed to it. She is then less likely to try to have her litter under the front porch or in the middle of your bed.

The box should have a wooden floor. Sides should be high enough to keep the puppies in but low enough to allow the mother to get out after she has fed them. Layers of newspapers spread over the whole area will make excellent bedding and will be absorbent enough to keep the surface warm and dry. They should be removed when wet or soiled and replaced with another thick layer. An old quilt or blanket is more comfortable for the mother and makes better footing for the nursing puppies, at least during the first week, than slippery newspaper. The quilt should be secured firmly.

SUPPLIES TO HAVE ON HAND

As soon as you have the whelping box prepared, set up the nursery by collecting the various supplies you will need when the puppies arrive. You should have the following items on hand: a box lined with towels for the puppies, a heating pad or hot water bottle to keep the puppy box warm, a pile of clean terrycloth towels or washcloths to remove membranes and to dry puppies, a stack of folded newspapers, a roll of paper towels, vaseline, rubber gloves, soap, iodine, muzzle, cotton balls, a small pair of blunt scissors to cut umbilical cords (stick them into an open bottle of alcohol so they keep freshly sterilized), a rectal thermometer, white thread, a flashlight in case the electricity goes off, a waste container, and a scale for weighing each puppy at birth.

It is necessary that the whelping room be warm and free from drafts, because puppies are delivered wet from the mother. Keep a little notebook and pencil handy so you can record the duration of the first labor and the time between the arrival of each puppy. If there is trouble in whelping, this is the information that the veterinarian will want. Keep his telephone number handy in case you have to call him in an emergency, and warn him to be prepared for an emergency, should you need him.

WHELPING

Be prepared for the actual whelping several days in advance. Usually the female will tear up papers, try to dig nests, refuse food, and generally act restless and nervous. These may be false alarms; the real test is her temperature, which will drop to below 100° about twelve hours before whelping. Take her temperature rectally at a set time each day, starting about a week before she is due to whelp. After her temperature goes down, keep her constantly with you or put her in the whelping box and stay in the room with her. She will seem anxious and look to you for reassurance. Be prepared to remove the membranes covering the puppy's head if the mother fails to do this, for the puppy could smother otherwise.

The mother should start licking the puppy as soon as it is out of the sac, thus drying and stimulating it, but if she does not perform this task you can do it with a soft rough towel, instead. The afterbirth should follow the birth of each puppy, attached to the puppy by the umbilical cord. Watch to make sure that each is expelled, for retaining this material can cause infection. The mother probably will eat the afterbirth after biting the cord. One or two will not hurt her; they stimulate milk supply as well as labor for remaining puppies. Too many, however, can make her lose her appetite for the food she needs to feed her puppies and regain her strength, so remove the rest of them along with the soiled newspapers, and keep the box dry and clean to relieve her anxiety.

If a puppy does not start breathing, wrap him in a towel, hold him upside down with his head toward the ground, and shake him vigorously. If he still does not breathe, rub his ribs briskly; if this also fails, administer artificial respiration by compressing the ribs about twenty times per minute.

If the mother does not bite the cord, or bites it too close to the body, you should take over the job to prevent an umbilical hernia. Cut the cord a short distance from the body with your blunt scissors. Put a drop of iodine on the end of the cord; it will dry up and fall off in a few days.

The puppies should follow each other at regular intervals, but deliveries can be as short as five minutes or as long as two hours apart. A puppy may be presented backwards; if the mother does not seem to be in trouble, do not interfere. But if enough of the puppy is outside the birth canal, use a rough towel and help her by pulling gently on the puppy. Pull only when she pushes. A rear-first, or breech, birth can cause a puppy to strangle on its own umbilical cord, so don't let the mother struggle too long. Breech birth is quite common.

When you think all the puppies have been whelped, have your veterinarian examine the mother to determine if all the afterbirths have been expelled. He will probably give her an injection to be certain that the uterus is clean, a shot of calcium for prevention of eclampsia, and possibly an injection of penicillin to prevent infection.

RAISING THE PUPPIES

Hold each puppy to a breast as soon as you have dried him. This will be an opportunity to have a good meal without competition. Then place him in the small box that you have prepared so he will be out of his mother's way while she is whelping. Keep a record of birth weights and take weekly readings thereafter so that you will have an accurate account of the puppies' growth. After the puppies have arrived, take the mother outside for a walk and a drink, and then leave her to take care of them. Offer her a dish of vanilla ice cream or milk with corn syrup in it. She usually will eat lying down while the puppies are nursing and will appreciate the coolness of the ice cream during warm weather or in a hot room. She will not want to stay away from her puppies more than a minute or two the first few weeks. Be sure to keep water available at all times, and feed her milk or broth frequently, as she needs liquids to produce milk. To encourage her to eat, offer her the foods she likes best, until she "asks" to be fed without your tempting her. She will soon develop a ravenous appetite and should be fed whenever she is hungry.

Be sure that all the puppies are getting enough to eat. Cut their claws with special dog "nail" clippers, as they grow rapidly and scratch the mother as the puppies nurse. Normally the puppies should be completely weaned by six weeks, although you may start to give them supplementary feedings at three weeks. They will find it easier to lap semi-solid food.

As the puppies grow up, the mother will go into the box only to nurse them, first sitting up and then standing. To dry up her milk supply completely, keep her away from her puppies for longer periods. After a few days of part-time nursing she will be able to stay away for much longer periods of time, and then completely. The little milk left will be resorbed.

When the puppies are five weeks old, consult your veterinarian about temporary shots to protect them against distemper and hepatitis; it is quite possible for dangerous infectious germs to reach them even though you keep their living quarters sanitary. You can expect the puppies to need at least one worming before they are ready to go to their new homes, so take a stool sample to your veterinarian before they are three weeks old. If one puppy has worms, all should be wormed. Follow your veterinarian's advice.

The puppies may be put outside, unless it is too cold, as soon as their eyes are open (about ten days), and they will benefit from the sunlight. A rubber mat or newspapers underneath their box will protect them from cold or dampness.

HOW TO TAKE CARE OF A LARGE LITTER

The size of a litter varies greatly. If your bitch has a large litter she may have trouble feeding all of the puppies. You can help her by preparing an extra puppy box. Leave half the litter with the mother and the other half in a warm place, changing their places at two-hour intervals at first. Later you may change them less frequently, leaving them all together except during the day. Try supplementary feeding, too, as soon as their eyes are open.

CAESAREAN SECTION

If your female goes into hard labor and is not able to give birth within two hours, you will know that there is something wrong. Call your veterinarian for advice. Some females must have Caesarean sections (taking puppies from the mother by surgery), but don't be alarmed if your dog has to undergo this. The operation is relatively safe. She can be taken to the veterinarian, operated on, and then be back in her whelping box at home within three hours, with all puppies nursing normally a short time later.

8. Health

WATCHING YOUR PUPPY'S HEALTH

First, don't be frightened by the number of diseases a dog can contract. The majority of dogs never get any of them. Don't become a dog-hypochondriac. All dogs have days when they feel lazy and want to lie around doing nothing. For the few diseases that you might be concerned about, remember that your veterinarian is your dog's best friend. When you first get your puppy, select a veterinarian who you feel is qualified to treat dogs. He will get to know your dog and will be glad to have you consult him for advice. A dog needs little medical care, but that little is essential to his good health and well-being. He needs:

1. Proper diet at regular hours
2. Clean, roomy housing
3. Daily exercise
4. Companionship and love
5. Frequent grooming
6. Regular check-ups by your veterinarian

THE USEFUL THERMOMETER

Almost every serious ailment shows itself by an increase in the dog's body temperature. If your dog acts lifeless, looks dull-eyed, and gives the impression of illness, check his temperature by using a rectal thermometer. Hold the dog and insert the thermometer, which should be lubricated with vaseline, and take a reading. The average normal temperature is 101.5° F. Excitement may raise this value slightly, but any rise of more than a few points is a cause for alarm. Consult your veterinarian.

FIRST AID

In general, a dog will heal his wounds by licking them. If he swallows anything harmful, chances are that he will throw it up. But it will probably make you feel better to help him if he is hurt, so treat his wounds as you would your own. Wash out the dirt and apply an antiseptic. If you are afraid that your dog has swallowed poison and you can't get to the veterinarian fast enough, try to induce vomiting by giving him a strong solution of salt water or mustard and water. Amateur diagnosis is dangerous, because the symptoms of so many dog diseases are alike. Too many people wait too long to take their dog to the doctor.

IMPORTANCE OF INOCULATIONS

With the proper series of inoculations, your dog will be almost completely protected against disease. However, it occasionally happens that the shot does not take, and sometimes a different form of the virus appears against which your dog may not be protected.

DISTEMPER

Probably the most virulent of all dog diseases is distemper. Young dogs are most susceptible to it, although it may affect dogs of all ages. The dog will lose his appetite, seem depressed, chilled, and run a fever. Often he will have a watery discharge from his eyes and nose. Unless treated promptly, the disease goes into advanced stages with infections of the lungs, intestines, and nervous system, and dogs that recover may be left with some impairment such as paralysis, convulsions, a twitch, or some other defect, usually spastic in nature. The best protection against this is very early inoculation with a series of permanent shots and a booster shot each year thereafter.

HEPATITIS

Veterinarians report an increase in the spread of this viral disease in recent years, usually with younger dogs as the victims. The initial symptoms — drowsiness, vomiting, great thirst, loss of appetite, and a high temperature — closely resemble those of distemper. These symptoms are often accompanied by swellings of the head, neck, and abdomen. The disease strikes quickly; death may occur in just a few hours. Protection is afforded by injection with a vaccine recently developed.

LEPTOSPIROSIS

This disease is caused by bacteria that live in stagnant or slow-moving water. It is carried by rats and dogs; infection is begun by the dog's licking substances contaminated by the urine or feces of infected animals. The symptoms are diarrhea and a yellowish-brown discoloration of the jaws, tongue, and teeth, caused by an inflammation of the kidneys. This disease can be cured if caught in time, but it is best to ward it off with a vaccine which your veterinarian can administer along with the distemper shots.

RABIES

This is an acute disease of the dog's central nervous system. It is spread by infectious saliva transmitted by the bite of an infected animal. Rabies is generally manifested in one of two classes of symptoms. The first is "furious rabies," in which the dog shows a period of melancholy or depression, then irritation, and finally paralysis. The first period lasts from a few hours to several days. During this time the dog is cross and will change his position often. He loses his appetite for food and begins to lick, bite, and swallow foreign objects. During the irritative phase the dog is spasmodically wild and has impulses to run away. He acts in a fearless manner and runs and bites at everything in sight. If he is caged or confined he will fight at the bars, often breaking teeth or fracturing his jaw. His bark becomes a peculiar howl. In the final, or paralytic, stage, the animal's lower jaw becomes paralyzed and hangs down; he walks with a stagger and saliva drips from his mouth. Within four to eight days after the onset of paralysis, the dog dies.

The second class of symptoms is referred to as "dumb rabies" and is characterized by the dog's walking in a bearlike manner, head down. The lower jaw is paralyzed and the dog is unable to bite. Outwardly it may seem as though he had a bone caught in his throat.

Even if your pet should be bitten by a rabid dog or other animal, he probably can be saved if you get him to the veterinarian in time for a series of injections. However, after the symptoms have appeared no cure is possible. But remember that an annual rabies inoculation is almost certain protection against rabies. If you suspect your dog of rabies, notify your local Health Department. A rabid dog is a danger to all who come near him.

COUGHS, COLDS, BRONCHITIS, PNEUMONIA

Respiratory diseases may affect the dog because he is forced to live under man-made conditions rather than in his natural environment. Being subjected to cold or a draft after a bath, sleeping near an air conditioner or in the path of a fan or near a radiator can cause respiratory ailments. The symptoms are similar to those in humans. The germs of these diseases, however, are different and do not affect both dogs and humans, so they cannot be infected by each other. Treatment is much the same as for a child with the same type of illness. Keep the dog warm, quiet, and well fed. Your veterinarian has antibiotics and other remedies to help the dog recover.

INTERNAL PARASITES

There are four common internal parasites that may infect your dog. These are roundworms, hookworms, whipworms, and tapeworms. The first three can be diagnosed by laboratory examination; the presence of tapeworms is determined by seeing segments in the stool or attached to the hair around the tail. Do not under any circumstances attempt to worm your dog without the advice of your veterinarian. After first determining what type of worm or worms are present, he will advise you of the best method of treatment.

EXTERNAL PARASITES

The dog that is groomed regularly and provided with clean sleeping quarters should not be troubled by fleas, ticks, or lice. If the dog should become infested with any of these parasites, he should be treated with a medicated dip bath or the new oral medications that are presently available.

SKIN AILMENTS

Any persistent scratching may indicate an irritation. Whenever you groom your dog, look for the reddish spots that may indicate eczema, mange, or fungal infection. Rather than treating your dog yourself, take him to the

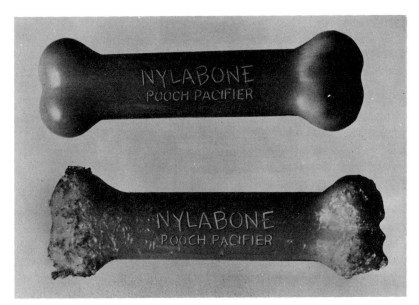

NYLABONE® is a necessity that is available at your local petshop (not in supermarkets). The puppy or grown dog chews the hambone flavored nylon into a frilly dog toothbrush, massaging his gums and cleaning his teeth as he plays. Veterinarians highly recommend this product . . . but beware of cheap imitations which might splinter or break.

veterinarian, as some of the conditions may be difficult to eradicate and can cause permanent damage to his coat.

EYES, EARS, TEETH, AND CLAWS

If you notice foreign matter collecting in the corners of your dog's eyes, wipe it out with a piece of cotton or tissue. If there is a discharge, check with your veterinarian.

Examine your dog's ears daily. Remove all visible wax, using a piece of cotton dipped in a boric acid solution or a solution of equal parts of water and hydrogen peroxide. Be gentle and don't probe into the ear, but just clean the parts you can see.

Don't give your dog bones to chew: they can choke him or puncture his intestines. Today veterinarians and dog experts recommend Nylabone, a synthetic bone manufactured by a secret process, that can't splinter or break even when pounded by a hammer. Nylabone will keep puppies from chewing furniture, aid in relieving the aching gums of a teething pup, and act as a toothbrush for the older dog, preventing the accumulation of tartar. Check your dog's mouth regularly and, as he gets older, have your veterinarian clean his teeth twice a year.

To clip your dog's claws, use specially designed clippers that are available at your petshop. Never take off too much of the claw, as you might

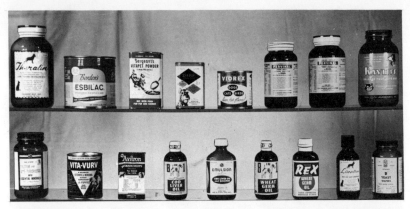

Active dogs and breeding bitches need food supplements. Visit your petshop for fresh vitamins and minerals to be added to your dog's diet.

cut the quick, which is sensitive and will bleed. Be particularly careful when you cut claws in which the quick is not visible. If you have any doubts about being able to cut your dog's claws, have your veterinarian or petshop do it periodically.

CARE OF THE AGED DOG

With the increased knowledge and care available, there is no reason why your dog should not live to a good old age. As the years go by he may need a little additional care. Remember that an excessively fat dog is not healthy, particularly as he grows older, so limit the older dog's food accordingly. He needs exercise as much as ever, although his heart cannot bear the strain of sudden and violent exertion. Failing eyesight or hearing means lessened awareness of dangers, so you must protect him more than ever.

Should you decide at this time to get a puppy, to avoid being without a dog when your old friend is no longer with you, be very careful how you introduce the puppy. He naturally will be playful and will expect the older dog to respond to his advances. Sometimes the old dog will get a new lease on life from a new puppy, but he may be consumed with jealousy. Do not give the newcomer the attention that formerly was exclusively the older dog's. Feed them apart, and show your old friend that you still love him the most; the puppy, not being accustomed to individual attention, will not mind sharing your love.

9. Showing

There is no greater pleasure for the owner than showing a beautiful dog perfectly groomed and trained for the show ring. Whether he wins or not, it is gratifying to show a dog in superb condition, one that is a credit to your training and care. A great deal of preparation, both for you and your dog, is needed before the day that you do any serious winning. Showing is not so easy as it looks, even if you have a magnificent dog. He must be presented to the judge so that all of his good points are shown to advantage. This requires practice in gaiting, daily grooming from puppyhood, and the proper diet to make him sound in body.

When you buy your puppy you probably will think he is the best in the country and possibly in the world, but before you enter the highly competitive world of dog shows, get some unbiased expert opinion. As your dog matures, compare him with the standard of his breed. Visit a few dog shows as a spectator and make mental notes of what is required of the handlers and dogs. Watch how the experienced handlers manage their dogs to bring out their best points.

TYPES OF DOG SHOWS

There are various types of dog shows. The American Kennel Club sanctioned matches are shows at which purebred dogs may compete, but not for championship points. These are excellent for you to enter to accustom you and your dog to showing. If your dog places in a few match shows, then you might seriously consider entering the big-time shows. An American Kennel Club all-breed show is one at which purebred dogs compete for championship points. An American Kennel Club specialty show is for one breed only. It may be held in conjunction with an all-breed show (by designating the classes at that show as its specialty show) or it may be held entirely apart. Obedience trials are different in that in them the dog is judged according to his obedience and ability to perform, not by his conformation to the breed standard.

There are two types of championship conformation shows: *benched* and *unbenched*. At a benched show your dog must be on his appointed bench during the advertised hours of the show's duration. He may be removed from the bench only to be taken to the exercise pen or to be groomed (an hour before showing) in an area designated for handlers to set up their crates and grooming tables. At an unbenched show your car may serve as a bench for your dog.

To become a champion your dog must win fifteen points in competition with other dogs; a portion of the fifteen points must be awarded as major point wins (three to five points) under different judges.

HOW TO ENTER

If your dog is purebred and registered with the AKC — or eligible for registration — you may enter him in the appropriate show class for which his age, sex, and previous show record qualify him. You will find coming shows listed in the different dog magazines or at your petshop. Write to the secretary of the show, asking for the premium list. When you receive the entry form, fill it in carefully and send it back with the required entry fee. Then, before the show, you should receive your exhibitor's pass, which will admit you and your dog to the show. Here are the five official show classes:

PUPPY CLASS: Open to dogs at least six months and not more than twelve months of age. Limited to dogs whelped in the United States and Canada.

NOVICE CLASS: Open to dogs six months of age or older that have never won a first prize in any class other than the puppy class, and less than three first prizes in the novice class itself. Limited to dogs whelped in the United States or Canada.

BRED BY EXHIBITOR CLASS: Open to all dogs, except champions, six months of age or over which are exhibited by the same person, or his immediate family, or kennel that was the recognized breeder on the records of the American Kennel Club.

AMERICAN-BRED CLASS: Open to dogs that are not champions, six months of age or over, whelped in the United States after a mating which took place in the United States.

OPEN CLASS: Open to dogs six months of age or over, with no exceptions.

In addition there are local classes, the Specials Only class, and brace and team entries.

For full information on dog shows, read the book *HOW TO SHOW YOUR OWN DOG,* by Virginia Tuck Nichols. (T.F.H.)

ADVANCED PREPARATION

Before you go to a show your dog should be trained to gait at a trot beside you, with head up and in a straight line. In the ring you will have to gait your dog around the edge with other dogs and then individually up and down the center runner. In addition the dog must stand for examination by the judge, who will look at him closely and feel his head and body structure. He should be taught to stand squarely, hind feet slightly back, head up on the alert. Showing requires practice training sessions in advance. Get a friend to act as judge and set the dog up and "show" him a few minutes every day.

Sometime before the show, give your dog a bath so he will look his best. Get together all the things you will need to take to the show. You will want to take a water dish and a bottle of water for your dog (so he won't be affected by a change in drinking water). Take your show lead, bench chain (if it is a benched show), combs and brush, and the identification ticket sent by the show superintendent, noting the time you must be there and the place where the show will be held, as well as the time of judging.

THE DAY OF THE SHOW

Don't feed your dog the morning of the show, or give him at most a light meal. He will be more comfortable in the car on the way, and will show more enthusiastically. When you arrive at the show grounds, find out where he is to be benched and settle him there. Your bench or stall number is on your identification ticket, and the breed name will be on placards fastened to the ends of the row of benches. Once you have your dog securely fastened to his stall by a bench chain (use a bench crate instead of a chain if you prefer), locate the ring where your dog will be judged (the number and time of showing will be on the program of judging which came with your ticket). After this you may want to take your dog to the exercise ring to relieve himself, and give him a small drink of water. Your dog will have been groomed before the show, but give him a final brushing just before going into the show ring. When your breed judging is called, it is your responsibility to be at the ringside ready to go in. The steward will give you an armband which has on it the number of your dog.

Then, as you step into the ring, try to keep your knees from knocking! Concentrate on your dog and before you realize it you'll be out again, perhaps back with the winners of each class for more judging and finally, with luck, it will be over and you'll have a ribbon and trophy.

ENCYCLOPEDIA OF DOG BREEDS, by Ernest H. Hart. This is the most complete all-breed dog book ever written. Every recognized breed as well as many that are virtually unknown in America is illustrated and discussed. The book contains six large color sections and a wealth of black and white photos and line drawings. History, management and care of all dogs is included along with new and fascinating breed information. This

classic in canine literature is available at your pet shop or book store. Published by T.F.H. Publications.

BIBLIOGRAPHY

Breed Your Dog, Dr. Leon Whitney, 64 pp., $1.00. Illustrated throughout with instructive photographs in both color and black and white. Covers aspects of breeding through puppyhood.

Dollars In Dogs, Leon F. Whitney, D.V.M., 255 pp., $6 95. Twenty-six chapters on different vocations in the vast field of dog business. An excellent book for your library.

First Aid For Your Dog, Dr. Herbert Richards, 64 pp., $1.00. Illustrated throughout in both color and black and white.

Groom Your Dog, Leon F. Whitney, D.V.M., 64 pp., $1.00. Illustrated throughout with both color and black and white photographs showing various grooming techniques.

How To Feed Your Dog, Dr. Leon F. Whitney, 64 pp., $1.00. Best diets and feeding routines for puppies and adult canines. Profusely illustrated in color and black and white.

How To Housebreak And Train Your Dog, Arthur Liebers, 80 pp., $1.00. Six educational chapters on training your dog. Illustrated in color and black and white photographs.

How To Raise And Train A Pedigreed Or Mixed Breed Puppy, Arthur Liebers, 64 pp., $1.00. Nine chapters covering such canine questions as choosing your puppy through breeding the adult. Illustrated in both color and black and white photographs.

How To Show Your Dog, Virginia Tuck Nichols, 252 pp., $6.95. This book is written for the novice who plans to show his dog. An excellent text to make your dog library complete.

The Distemper Complex, Leon F. Whitney, D.V.M., and George D. Whitney, D.V.M., 219 pp., $6.95. A comprehensive canine health book. Nineteen revealing chapters. A thirty-nine-page bibliography. Completely indexed.

This Is The Puppy, Ernest Hart, 190 pp., $6.95. Eleven profusely-illustrated chapters to guide the reader in the care and selection of a puppy. Full-color photographs. Also black and white candids. Indexed.